HOW HAS
COVID-19
CHANGED OUR WORLD?

By Kara L. Laughlin

childsworld.com

Published by The Child's World®
1980 Lookout Drive
Mankato, MN 56003-1705
800-599-READ
www.childsworld.com

Photos ©: Aleksandra Suzi/
Shutterstock.com: 22;
Cryptographer/Shutterstock.com: 9;
FamVeld/Shutterstock.com: 18; Kris
Cavada/Shutterstock.com: cover,
2; PhotobyTawat/Shutterstock.com:
20; Picturesque Japan/Shutterstock.
com: 17; Prostock-studio/
Shutterstock.com: 5; Robi Jaffrey/
Shutterstock.com: 15; settsunokami/
Shutterstock.com: 12; Sviatlana
Yankouskaya/Shutterstock.com: 6;
Unai Huizi/Shutterstock.com: 11

ISBN 9781503853171
(Reinforced Library Binding)

ISBN 9781503853218
(Portable Document Format)

ISBN 9781503853270
(Online Multi-user eBook)

LCCN: 2020939117

Printed in the United
States of America

About the Author
Kara Laughlin lives in Leesburg, VA with her husband, three kids, and a dog. She has written over 50 nonfiction books for children.

CONTENTS

CHAPTER ONE

COVID-19 Changes Everything

What did you do on New Year's Eve 2019? Did you have a party? Watch TV? In Wuhan, China, scientists were studying a new **virus**. It had made dozens of people very sick. Soon it would sicken people all across the world, causing a global **pandemic**. The virus was COVID-19.

By June of 2020, COVID-19 had spread through the world. It infected more than six million people and killed nearly 380,000.

Symptoms of COVID-19 include fever, cough, difficulty breathing, and body aches.

With schools closed,
children everywhere
began learning from home.

Soon nations were calling for **social distancing** to slow the virus. People stayed at home. Parties were canceled. Most public places closed. People started wearing masks in public. Schools closed. Graduations were canceled. Weddings were postponed. Many nursing homes closed to visitors. Social distancing did a good job of slowing COVID-19. But it came at a cost.

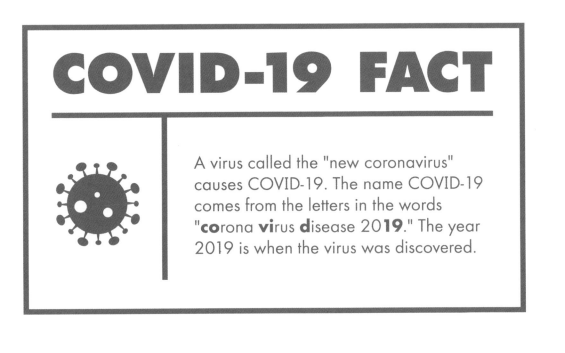

COVID-19 FACT

A virus called the "new coronavirus" causes COVID-19. The name COVID-19 comes from the letters in the words "**co**rona **vi**rus **d**isease 20**19**." The year 2019 is when the virus was discovered.

CHAPTER TWO

A Balancing Act

COVID-19 has hurt the **economy**. Many businesses have closed. Some will not reopen. Airlines, restaurants, and hotels lost most of their customers. Millions of people lost their jobs. In the US, more people are out of work than any time since the **Great Depression**.

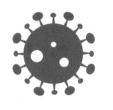

The United States confirmed its first case of COVID-19 on January 20, 2020.

In April of 2020, the unemployment rate in the United States reached 14.7 percent. That was an all-time high— it meant that nearly 1 in every 15 people did not have a job.

World leaders are working hard to slow COVID-19 *and* help the economy. It is tough to do both at once. Opening businesses too soon risks more people getting sick. But waiting too long keeps people from earning the money they need. Leaders are trying to strike a balance.

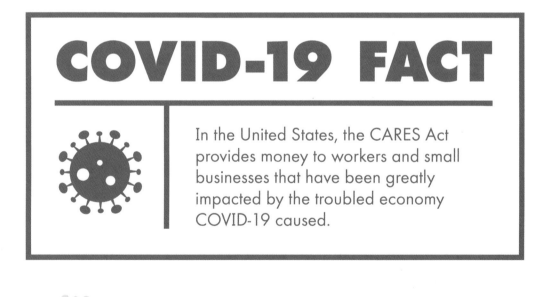

COVID-19 FACT

In the United States, the CARES Act provides money to workers and small businesses that have been greatly impacted by the troubled economy COVID-19 caused.

Re-opening hair salons during COVID-19 is difficult. People cannot social distance as they should when someone is washing or cutting their hair. Shop owners and customers must take extra steps to keep everyone safe.

Without the usual tourists crowding the area, these deer walked down a street in Japan.

CHAPTER THREE

COVID-19 and the Environment

COVID-19 has also changed the environment. Fewer airplanes are flying. Many factories are closed. People are driving less. In many cities, the air is cleaner. The water is clearer. People can hear birds instead of traffic. Wild animals walk down the street.

Most experts think these changes won't slow **climate change**. They expect pollution levels to rise again when cities fully reopen.

Others are more hopeful. People like seeing more animals. They like the quiet, clean cities. Maybe they will fight to keep them. COVID-19 forced the world to make huge changes in a very short time. Now we know that quick changes are possible. Maybe we can make big changes to fight climate change, too.

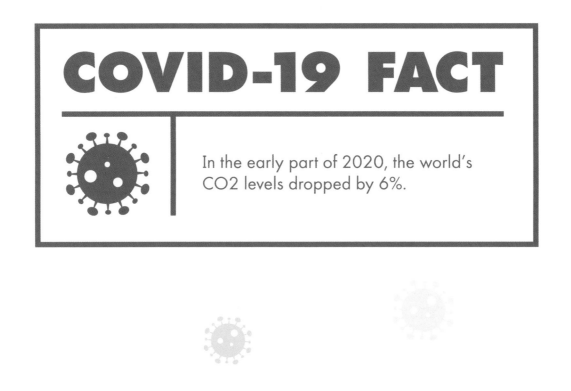

COVID-19 FACT

In the early part of 2020, the world's CO_2 levels dropped by 6%.

New York City's Central Park is normally bustling with people. COVID-19 has made it a very quiet place.

CHAPTER FOUR

The New Normal

Living with COVID-19 can be hard. People everywhere just want their lives to return to normal. But many changes brought by COVID-19 are here for a while. Some might even be here to stay. We will need to get used to a "new normal."

COVID-19 FACT

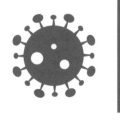

The World Health Organization (WHO) uses the phrase 'physical distancing' to remind people to stay socially close. Staying in touch with friends and family keeps us healthy!

Before COVID-19, most people shook hands. Now people either wave or touch elbows. This might be the way we greet one another from now on.

Wearing masks in public places might be something people do from now on. The masks keep germs from spreading.

It can take time to find a "new normal." You may feel sad, scared, or angry for a long time. Talking with an adult can help. After all, living through the COVID-19 pandemic has changed you too. Have you had to be extra patient? Strong? Brave? Those things change us on the inside. They help us grow.

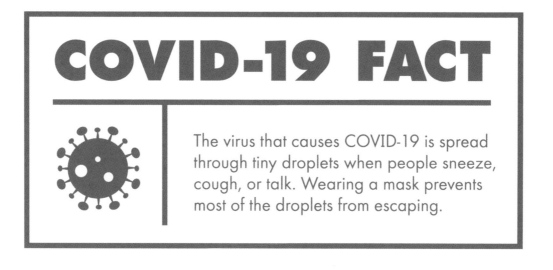

COVID-19 FACT

The virus that causes COVID-19 is spread through tiny droplets when people sneeze, cough, or talk. Wearing a mask prevents most of the droplets from escaping.

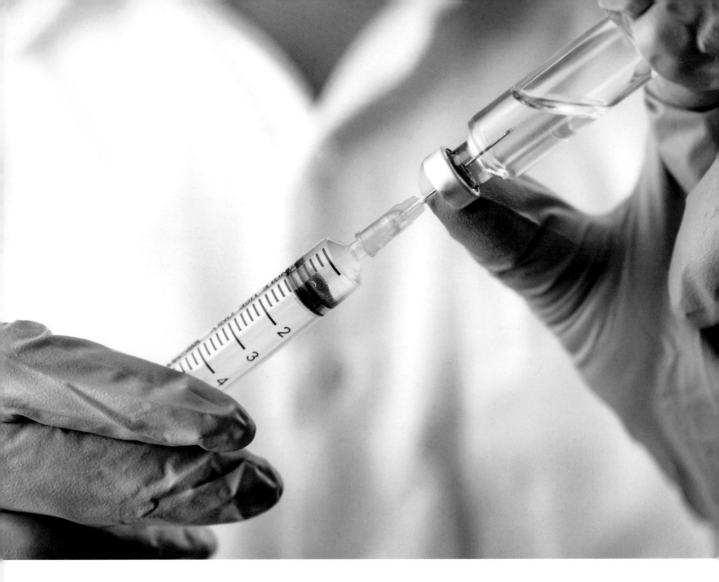

Scientists are working hard to find a **vaccine** for
COVID-19. It may take months or years, but researchers
aren't giving up. People are taking care of those harmed by
COVID-19. Friends and neighbors are working hard to stop
the spread of the disease. Families are trying to find a new
normal. Those things won't change!

THINK ABOUT IT

There are lots of things you can do at home while keeping yourself and others safe.

Get to Know a Helper. Do you know anyone helping those hurt by COVID-19? Make a list of the helpers you know. Talk to someone on your list. Ask them about how they help. Maybe you will get an idea for how you can help, too!

Grow Hope. When money is tight, fresh vegetables are hard to get. In the 1930's, people planted "victory gardens" to help with shortages caused by war. Try planting your own "victory garden." If you end up with extra veggies, donate them to a food bank.

Change How You See It. How has COVID-19 changed you? Make a list of changes you don't like. Then make a list of changes for the better. Maybe you miss your friends (bad list), but you are spending more time with your family (good list). Share your lists with an adult. Talk about ways to create good changes from the bad list. For example, if you miss going out for ice cream, you could learn to make it at home.

Special days still come when there's a global pandemic. People have found creative ways to celebrate when they can't be together. Many people are using the Internet to connect with friends and family. Schools are holding online graduations. Couples are live-streaming weddings as guests watch on their computers. People aren't letting COVID-19 stop their celebrations!

GLOSSARY

climate change (KLY-mut CHAYNJ) Climate change is the change in an area's normal climate conditions (such as rain and temperature) over a long period of time.

economy (ih-KON-uh-mee) A country's economy is the way it runs its businesses, trade, and finances.

Great Depression (GRAYT dih-PRESH-un) The Great Depression was a time in the 1930s when the economy was greatly troubled. Many people were out of work, hungry, and homeless.

pandemic (pan-DEM-ik): A pandemic is an illness that has spread all over the world. COVID-19 became a pandemic in 2020.

social distancing (SOH-shull DIH-stan-sing) Social distancing is a way to stop the spread of a disease. It involves keeping at least six feet (2 m) away from other people, or staying at home.

vaccine (vak-SEEN) A vaccine is a weakened or dead form of a disease that is swallowed or injected into a person. This causes their body to fight the germs, and gives them the ability to fight that disease's germs if the body comes in contact with them again.

virus (VY-russ) A virus is a very tiny germ that causes diseases. A virus can only be seen with a special kind of microscope.

TO LEARN MORE

IN THE LIBRARY

Larson, Jennifer S. *What Is Money, Anyway?: Why Dollars and Coins Have Value.* Minneapolis, MN: Lerner, 2010.

Latta, Sara. *What is COVID-19?* Mankato, MN: The Child's World, 2021.

Wallace, Adam M. *The Day My Kids Stayed Home: Explaining COVID-19 and the Corona Virus to Your Kids.* Adam M. Wallace, 2020.

ON THE WEB

Visit our website for links about COVID-19:

childsworld.com/links

Note to Parents, Teachers, and Librarians: We routinely verify our Web links to make sure they are safe and active sites. So encourage your readers to check them out!

INDEX